faces of the
EASTERN SHORE

This book is dedicated to the memory of my parents,
Mildred and Albert A. Van Riper

....

FIRST EDITION

ISBN 1-56566-012-9
LIBRARY OF CONGRESS CATALOGUE CARD NUMBER 92-80364

DISTRIBUTED BY: THOMASSON-GRANT
ONE MORTON DRIVE, CHARLOTTESVILLE, VIRGINIA
804-977-1780

PUBLISHED BY: QUESADA HOUSE. WASHINGTON D.C.
BOOK DESIGN BY: PAT MARSHALL DESIGN, INC.

PRINTED IN JAPAN BY DAI NIPPON

faces of the
EASTERN SHORE

Photographs and Text
By
Frank Van Riper

Foreword by James A. Michener

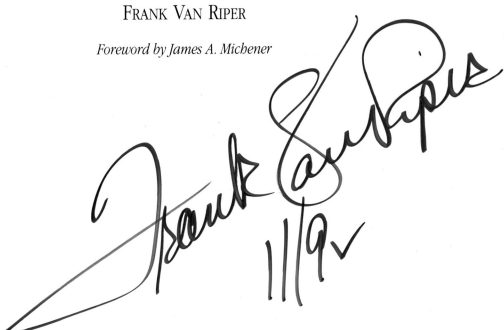

INTRODUCTION

About this time, the custom arose of referring to the Eastern Shore with capital letters, as if it were a special place; this tribute was never paid the western shore.

James A. Michener
Chesapeake

Many people in this book love the Eastern Shore—find it a special place— for its solitude and isolation. Some were born to this peace and take it for granted; others sought it out and cherish it. I am one of the others.

My first impression of the Eastern Shore—the largely rural communities of Maryland, Virginia and Delaware that make up the Delmarva Peninsula—was of Chincoteague Island, Virginia, during a cold winter's day more than ten years ago as my wife and I tried to help our friends Barbara and Sol figure out how they were going to refurbish the small house they had just bought and which they planned to use for long weekends and in retirement. When Judy and I first saw the place, on Church Street, near Main, it already had been gutted. By the time it was finished it was a treasure, its cozy parlor warmed by a woodburning stove.

What I remember most, though, were the telephones. Sol loved them. He collected old ones; he bought new ones. Since he was starting from scratch, he had phone jacks installed everywhere. And because Judy and I were visitors to this wonderful place, whenever the phone rang it was never for us. To a then-newspaper reporter like myself, whose daily professional life was shaped by a constantly ringing phone or teletype bell, this was a transforming event.

The ensuing years saw us visit Chincoteague and other places on the Eastern Shore regularly and grow even more comfortable with the slower pace and the singular people. And they, of course, are the reason for this book.

Separated by the Chesapeake Bay from the bustle of the mainland, and seemingly light years away from the hurried lifestyles of Washington, Baltimore and Annapolis, the Eastern Shore developed at its own pace and with its own identity. The people, especially those in the more out of the way rural areas that have names like Tangier, Hooper's, Parksley or Pocomoke, are different from their urban cousins—if they have any at all. (On the remotest spots like Tangier Island, Va., where people still speak in the accents of Devon and Cornwall, whole generations in the past lived and died without venturing across to the mainland, or sometimes even to the rest of the Eastern Shore.)

Though isolated, the Eastern Shore is not homogeneous, like say, Down East Maine. It is a racially mixed society, reflecting the impact of the booming slave trades of pre-colonial, colonial and Civil War times, and all the accompanying advantages and disadvantages are present today because of it. (As one might expect, tensions were high during the Civil War, with Union Maryland and Confederate Virginia in such close proximity. But nowhere higher than on

Chincoteague, Va., which voted 132 to 2 to remain in the Union throughout the war.)

It is a conservative region—some of the most conservative voting blocs in Maryland, for example, are on the Eastern Shore—though one of its most conservative cities, Crisfield, has elected a black Chief of Police.

It is a place that loves the land and the water, but often seems at a loss how to love them wisely. At this writing the controversy over how to Save the Bay persists with watermen on one side, ecologists on the other. One side sees meddling bureaucrats limiting one's ability to make a living; the other sees foolhardy locals ignoring the environmental calamity that lies literally at their feet. Some of the most intelligent reporting on this subject, reflecting credit on both sides, is by Tom Horton of the Baltimore Sun.

It was because of these sometimes contradictory things that I decided to record the Faces of the Eastern Shore—as well as have the faces talk to the reader in an accompanying text. My project began in April, 1990, as part of the American Society of Magazine Photographers "10,000 Eyes" project to mark the 150th birthday of photography, and ended nearly two years later. Almost without exception, everyone I approached let me take their picture and I am in their debt. I followed my nose—and the recommendations of others. Oftentimes, one of my subjects would suggest someone else to photograph, who would suggest someone else, etc., etc.

No thanks to those who helped make this book possible would be complete without a deep bow to those who patiently, graciously, stood in front of my camera.

Thanks also to Regina and Jonathan Hall, whose home on Chincoteague was our base of operations and who provided Judy and me with succor, shelter, food and laughter throughout. The two years on this project only deepened our friendship.

Barbara and Sol Orden, who introduced us to the Eastern Shore, helped us to grow close to the people in their community. If Sol insisted that he could never be considered a "Tigger" since he would always be from "away," the grief that his Chincoteague friends felt at his sudden death last year belied that. And every time I sit in front of that woodburning stove, I will honor his memory.

Elizabeth Frazier, Richard Snowden and William and Agnes Doeller all played a huge part in getting this project off the ground. Their skill and support cannot adequately be repaid.

In addition, I thank the following people for their timely suggestions, critical comments, wisdom and help: Lois Brown, the Chincoteague Volunteer Fire Department, the Chincoteague Wildlife Refuge, Cindy and John Chirtea, Octavian Cretu, Alec Dann, Corinne and Ted Davidov, Sheryl Denbo, Chief Willis J. Dize, Ron Fein, Deborah Gandy, Nancy and Carl Gewirz, Harry Hamburg, Marilyn Hannigan, Jim Harrison, Katherine Harting, Marilyn and Guy Henry, Davina Grace Hill, Gregory Holmes, Frank Jackman, Mark Jacoby, JoAnn Jones, R.E. Jones, Iris and Bill Kaufman, John Kings, Pat Marshall, James A. Michener, Neil Selkirk, Steve Silverman, Chief Harry Thornton, Dr. Ernst Wildi, Franklin Young and Earl Zubkoff.

Finally, there is Judy, my wife and partner, who traveled so many of these miles with me. I could never have done this book without her gentle laughter and her critical eye. I love her for both.

Frank Van Riper
Washington, DC
February, 1992

When a productive writer lives into his eighties he is besieged by friends and others he barely knows to write forewords for books they have written or are about to write. I receive about fifteen such invitations a year and obviously cannot comply with many, even when I might want to.

Interestingly, most of the applicants ask me to write a Forward or a Foreward or, occasionally, a Forword, betraying the fact that they have read little or failed to understand what they did read. In fact the wrong spelling has become so common that I have come to believe they know more than I do. What they want is a Forward, a kind of battle cry meaning: "Let's get done with this nonsense and hurry on to my writing." Perhaps dictionaries will modify their spelling of this word.

Rarely have I received a more inappropriate request than the one which led me to write this Forward. I did not know Frank Van Riper, had never heard of him. He sent with his request no letter of introduction from a mutual friend. He told me bluntly that my copy had to be in his hands by the end of December, five weeks away. And he closed with what read like a threat: "I look forward to hearing from you."

I thus had about six good reasons for declining, but he had been clever enough to send along with his peremptory request a sample of ten of his photographs, each accompanied by the literate and sensible explanatory text he proposed printing to accompany each portrait. The excellence attracted me but I was inclined to say no on the grounds that I did not know the author and had not the slightest obligation to help him.

But then I saw the photograph of the dozen-odd black men shucking oysters in Crisfield, Maryland and a wave of uncontrollable nostalgia swept over me, for I remember that rugged fishing village with a glow that will never die. This little town, population 2924, is known as the crab capital of Maryland's famed Eastern Shore, an area I have written about with affection. Each year they hold what is known as the Crisfield Crab Festival, and one time they invited me to serve as Grand Marshal of the affair. The choice was not unreasonable in that I had let it be known that I was making a field study trying to decide who in the region made the area's best crab cakes, a delicacy that the gods on Olympus would be glad to judge.

Among my duties as Marshal would be to sample some three dozen crab cakes and determine the winner, a job to which I looked forward with delight and salivation. But as the parade began, with me seated in the back seat of a well worn Pontiac, the organizers told me: "Don't be surprised, Mr. Michener, if they throw eggs or tomatoes at you. They aren't aiming at you. It's the mayor they want to get. He enraged us by insisting on riding beside you because he calculated they wouldn't dare throw at him, very unpopular man, with you sitting there and apt to be hit."

It was a chilly parade, and a silent one. No one cheered when I passed, but on the other hand, no one threw tomatoes either. The mayor was not assaulted but he did garner some hisses. The man driving the car leaned back and said: "Book critics, I think." However, when the time came to taste the crab cakes, one of America's finest inventions when done properly, I found myself giving eight or nine of them marks above eighty-five and two in the nineties. The women of Crisfield know how to use the crabs their husbands catch.

But I am fond of Crisfield for another reason,

and to understand why you must look again at the excellent photograph of the oyster shuckers. Notice that virtually all are black, a feature of Crisfield life where whites have one job and blacks another and rarely do the twain meet. Also see how superbly the photo shows the manner in which the feet of the workers are kept off the cold cement floor, and not by placing a mere board there, because that wouldn't do the trick. The cold would come right up through the wood. The white owner of the joint had gone to the expense of providing a cleverly built stall which protects both the shucker and his feet. Apparently blacks and whites may not work together in Crisfield, but they look out for one another, and in the crab picking contest which I also judged that day, a black woman with flying fingers won from a bevy of white wizards who picked so fast I couldn't follow them.

But the story about black-white relations in Crisfield that I cherish came when Maryland educators, in a rare show of common sense, which I applauded and aided, decided to merge a branch of the University of Maryland in Salisbury, ninety-five percent white, with a Negro college only a few miles to the south, ninety-five percent black. Reason dictated that the two should be combined, so did economics and the principles of good education.

I assumed that the union would go through since I could see no reason to oppose it, but suddenly the blacks of the area protested vigorously on grounds that caught my attention: "If we have to send our children to a standard type of big university in Salisbury, they will be submerged by the white majority. Our boys will never be able to be captain of the football team and our girls will never be able to become Homecoming Queen."

The blacks would not have been able to kill the decision to join the two schools had not the white families in Crisfield also launched powerful pressure to keep the black school alive. Their reasoning: "Black colleges keep tuition and social fees low. We want our boys and girls to go there. Because if they go to the big white college in Salisbury, first thing you know the college will want them to buy musical instruments so they can play in the band." And it was the whites of Crisfield who enabled the blacks to hold onto their little college. I like a place like that.

But I doubt I would have agreed to write this Forward because of my affection for Crisfield alone. My wife and I spent four happy years on Maryland's Eastern Shore. I did some of my better work there, made some of my firmest friends. We knew the men who sailed the famous skipjacks, and those who tong for oysters, one of the hardest jobs in the world, standing in a small boat on a windy bay when the temperature has plunged, and operating tongs whose handles are ten feet or longer, and probing the bottom for oysters, which you then raise to the surface by running your hands down the length of the icy-cold wet handles and bringing the bivalves into your boat. What a way to earn a living!

As I restudied the faces of the Eastern Shore people in Van Riper's photographs and saw the faces with which I had become so familiar when I worked there—the chicken feeders, the two lady morticians, the storekeeper, the judge—I felt as if I were back home, for he has caught the authentic look of this remarkable corner of America. And I thought: What this rascal has done is belatedly to illustrate my novel *Chesapeake*, and superbly. These are the people I wrote about, and I can't refuse his request.

So I submit this Forward in a new sense of the word: "Let's quit these niceties and rush forward into the book itself."

James A. Michener
Texas Center for Writers

It is cold, wet and boring work, shucking oysters, and no one has come up with a better way to do it than with two gloved hands and a wickedly sharp knife.

Like their brethren who pick crabs, oyster shuckers are paid piecework. That is, the amount of meat they produce determines how much they make. It is one reason there is little wasted motion on the line. The work begins at 7 a.m. or earlier and it can go—nonstop—until noon or later depending on the abundance of each day's catch.

Here in Crisfield the work has been steady but the veterans always worry about there being less today than yesterday. Sometimes they are right.

Shucking provides extra money for some; a livelihood for others. The movement of the knife into the hard rugged shell and under the precious oyster meat is fluid, even poetic, when done by a professional. It is awkward, even frightening, when done by an amateur. The work is best done standing and one concession to comfort is the wooden platform for each shucker, the better to keep away from the leg-aching concrete as well as to avoid the wet.

A shore bird can take an oyster in its beak, fly high with it, drop it on a rock, then swoop down to feast on the liberated meat. The human method really isn't much different, only more efficient.

Like his grandfather and namesake, Ira Hudson of Chincoteague, Va., is a duck carver, only Ira the younger's work has an antic, whimsical quality—much like Ira himself.

"Here, son, set yourself down," he says with a giggle as he and his dog Sambo invite you to the rooftop aerie Ira and his wife Frances have just finished, complete with swing, whirligigs, awning and, of course, carved birds. The rooftop deck, unlike anything you have seen before, is Ira's sanctuary, and he rocks himself contentedly on his swing, regaling you with stories of Chincoteague.

No one will ever confuse Ira's birds with those that command hundreds of dollars each at the Easton Waterfowl Festival. But Ira's pieces have a kind of primitive attraction that is obviously genuine— the work of a true Eastern Shore original.

Ira and Frances have lived on the Shore all their lives, raising a family and scraping by. They have retired now as custodians at the nearby school and Ira devotes much of his time to his collection, despite his failing eyesight.

The times when son Randy is home, he helps his father in his shop, refurbishing old furniture and helping around the house. Randy has had a sad series of run-ins with the law, belied by a gentle manner and easy smile. Asked to display his collection of tattoos, Randy bares his arms and suddenly glowers into the camera. Seconds later, he is back to laughing.

In an area where names like Bo, Scorchy and Bubba are common, it should be no surprise that one of the most prominent public officials ever to come from the Eastern Shore goes by the name "Hot Dog."

Lloyd L. (Hot Dog) Simpkins—so named at an early age by his father, ostensibly because of his son's love of hot dogs—began public life in 1951 when he was elected to the Maryland House of Delegates. That was one year before the Bay Bridge linked Simpkins' native Eastern Shore with the rest of the state, a move that is still lamented by some of Simpkins' constituents. Over the next four decades he held a number of state posts, finally serving as the Eastern Shore's chief administrative judge. He retired from the bench in 1990, one day before reaching the state's mandatory retirement age of 70.

"All a judge has to do to be a good judge is to be fair, be honest, have some compassion and a little bit of a mean streak," Simpkins once told an interviewer.

True, Hot Dog presented a baleful countenance when he sat for his portrait in the Princess Anne courthouse just a few months before his retirement. But the camera can lie. This, after all, was a man whose reputation as a gentle prankster and hellraiser has become part of Maryland political legend.

For example, years ago when he was in the House, Simpkins cured a fellow delegate who early every morning would rouse his fellow lodgers in their Annapolis rooming house by banging a wastebasket on the floor. Simpkins retaliated by pushing a basketful of lighted cherry bombs into the delegate's bathroom while the lawmaker was on the toilet.

"They say when they tore the building down years later you could still see Tom Lowe's fingernail marks going up the wall where he tried to climb before the bombs went off."

"I been smithin' for 17 years now," said John Austin Ellsworth as he showed off his new shop in Lewes, Del.—and as his visitor tried not to stare at Ellsworth's massive arms.

"The public was so interested in the blacksmithing part of it that I wanted to build a shop that was accessible to everyone, and also so I could do school groups."

Ellsworth's forge was several years in the making and it tries to recreate the look of an oldtime blacksmith shop—even down to the sawdust on the floor. But in fact, even a modern forge looks pretty much the way it did a century and a half ago—so little in smithing has changed over that time.

"Mainly I do restoration work for local houses. That's about it. It started out as a hobby and I got carried away."

Born in Ohio, Ellsworth originally gravitated to oceanography and wound up on the Eastern Shore where he joined a company based in Lewes. "They left and I stayed," he said matter-of-factly.

You can't help but think of the Longfellow poem when you look at Ellsworth—he really does have arms like iron bands.

"I had some third graders in here and one of the kids looked at me and said: 'can weak men be blacksmiths?'"

"I said they can start out that way, but it sort of comes with the job. You start swinging a hammer all day long and it just sort of grows on you."

"The Lord sent me here...it was not my idea," says Hattie Ewell, pastor of the storefront Trinity United Holy Church in Pocomoke City, Md.

As churches go, this is not the ritz. Ewell's pews are hand-me-downs; her curtains are bedsheets. The flowers adorning her pulpit are plastic. If you come to Trinity United expecting to hear frenzied testimony and joyful noise you may be disappointed. Hattie Ewell is a decidedly low-key churchwoman, an articulate seriousminded person who notes that she is better described as a pastor than as an evangelist.

"Maryland in view soon" was the message contained in a vision relayed to Ewell by her own pastor in Delaware three years ago—and Ewell was a reluctant recipient of the word. But when the call comes, one has to listen.

Since that time, Ewell has tried to lead a poor, predominantly black flock through the moral thickets of a community she has difficulty understanding. "The morals of alot of the people are alot different here," she says. "The people are much more treacherous here...it's like a haze of wickedness over this area."

Of course, many of the problems Ewell confronts—she cites fornication, adultery, troubled youth, excessive drinking—can be functions of poverty and ignorance as much as "wickedness." But Ewell still has little sympathy for those who cannot live by the simple dictum: "There is only one need, and that is for holy living and clean living."

The Salisbury Baptist Temple's drive-in passion play bears little resemblance to its progenitor in Oberammergau. The dialogue, written by Pastor Oren Perdue (no relation to the better known poultry merchant), is a curious but somehow charming blend of the music of King James and the vulgate. ("Don't I get any change?" asks one character after buying a sacrificial pigeon at the temple.) The dialogue is pre-recorded and broadcast in FM so that during a performance the faithful can listen on their radios and watch from their cars as the cast mouths the words and re-enacts the final days of Christ.

The setting is impressive: a manmade hillside a few hundred yards from the one-story church/school complex. It is adorned with a stage-set temple, cave, and marketplace—as well as a partially-concealed cherry picker on which Christ ascends to heaven at the play's end. (At Christmastime, the hundred or so members of the congregation take to the stage once more for the annual Christmas pageant, heralding Christ's birth.)

The chill March evening of these photographs Rev. Perdue was absent. During the previous night's rehearsal the horse he was riding shied suddenly, fell, and rolled on the Reverend, shattering his ankle. Following the dress rehearsal and before we took leave of Perdue's gentle congregation, we signed a huge get well card. (A hardy Christian soldier, Perdue made it to opening night in a wheelchair.)

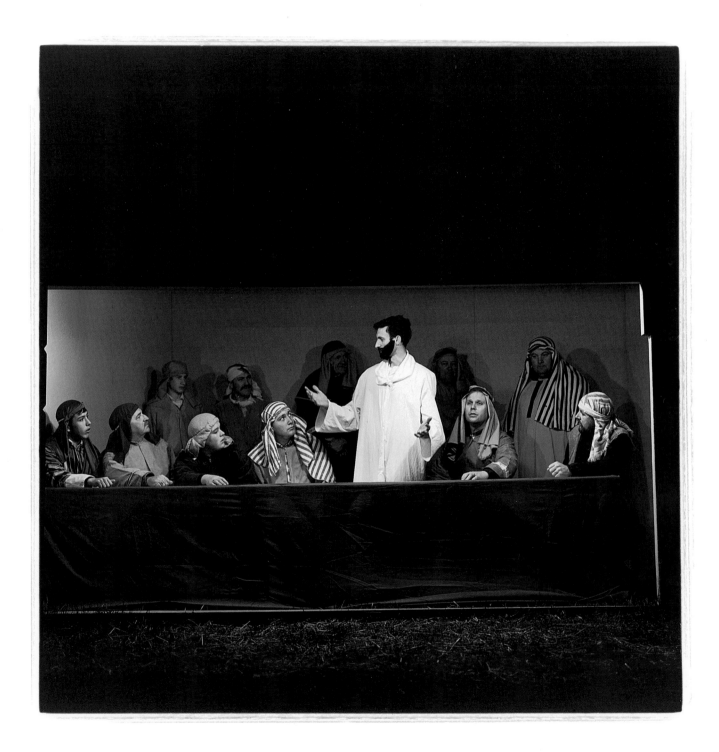

For Bill Paskey of Felton, Del., the attraction years ago was not to jets, Corvettes or Mack trucks, but to steam engines, diesels and big red cabooses. Bill Paskey was a train buff whose love of railroading didn't leave him when he grew up. In fact, when he grew up he decided to own the real thing.

Paskey makes his living as a farmer and originally developed a collector's eye for old steam-driven tractors. "Then I heard about a caboose up for sale in Reading, Pa., so I went up and put a sealed bid in—and I got it."

It was a 40-year-old beauty once run by the Pennsy, the old Pennsylvania Railroad, with the observation deck on top and to the rear. In other words, it was like every caboose stuck on the end of every kid's set of Lionels or American Flyers decades ago. And now Bill Paskey owned it.

He made a little junction for the caboose and the other gear he amassed—including an ancient luggage cart with equally ancient luggage piled upon it—then proceeded to fill the caboose with all kinds of stuff. "I just started collecting up train pictures and knickknacks and lanterns."

So now Bill Paskey has a mini-railroad museum just a few hundred yards away from his barns and feed pens. It's not really open to the public, but Bill and his helper Corky Corkell show it off to local school groups when the weather is warm.

Junk—good junk—is hard to find. But in Pocomoke City, Md., Trish Evans saves you a lot of trouble in her cluttered storefront a block off Main Street.

There one can wander (carefully, since there are hardly what you would call aisles) through hundreds of old treasures, the place redolent with the musty smell of someone's attic, where most of this stuff doubtless originated.

A Deco chandelier in need of a little work? It's there on that sofa in dire need of reupholstering. Old picture frames your passion? How about twelve or so over in the corner?

That Chesapeake Bay retriever strike your fancy? Forget it. That's Trish's and she wouldn't part with him for the world.

She is a cheerful soul, a rapid and enthusiastic talker who came to the Eastern Shore via Kansas, Pittsburgh, Black Mountain, N.C., and New York City. Her background is an odd mix of theater arts and business administration, and her career has seen her working on such arcane publications as the Journal of Corporate Ventures.

Trish came to the Eastern Shore out of medical necessity: in effect her doctors prescribed the move after she was struck by a car on Manhattan's Lexington Avenue. The accident left her temporarily blinded and suffering such severe trauma that a kidney was jeopardized because of the intrusion of bone fragments.

"They said I should live in a low-stress environment," Trish said, noting that the two places recommended to her were Somerset County Md., and anywhere in Maine.

She chose Pocomoke City, set up her "antiques" business and now just laughs when someone asks if her life is low-stress.

To a generation of Eastern Shore viewers Scorchy Tawes is a television legend. So is his jacket.

"If you're doing a book on the Eastern Shore," a friend said, "you've got to include Scorchy Tawes."

"What are scorchy tawes?" he was asked in dead earnest.

For want of a better description, Scorchy is a feature man, a color guy—someone whose stories on WBOC out of Salisbury document the sporting scene in an area that takes its sporting seriously. (So seriously, in fact, that anywhere you go on the Eastern Shore people refer to Scorchy as if he were an old friend. You can even mail order a videotape of his best stuff, just as you would country and western tapes or Genuine Diamond Rings from the home shopping channel.)

The name Tawes is as well known in Maryland politics as the name Perdue is in Maryland poultry. There was governor J. Millard Tawes, for example, and many other lesser lights of identical name. Scorchy, however, chose to make his name elsewhere.

"And if you do photograph Scorchy, tell him to wear the jacket." ("Could you wear the jacket, Scorchy?" "Sure.")

Showing up just outside of Crisfield, Scorchy had just come from covering a story and had his young cameraman in tow. Tawes was like a veteran hoofer. All he wanted to know was: where was his mark. A scenic spot with workboats in the background was found and Scorchy donned his jacket—a bright red nylon affair covered with patches from the many events he has covered or attended over the years.

He grabbed his fishing pole and hit his mark. The session lasted maybe ten minutes and Scorchy was gone, heading back to the studio to edit his tape.

Though baseball is a summer game, January, February and March are the best months for Fred Roser's batting cage in Trappe, Md.

"Harold Baines hits here every week in the winter," Roser said of the Oakland A's slugger who makes his home only a few miles from the "Sports Trappe" and who maintains his batting eye in the off-season by plastering machine-fired fastballs. Roser has operated his batting cage-cum-miniature golf course for more than four years but chuckles when asked if he makes a living at it.

He is an auto dealer and local rep for Peterbilt trucks. The Sports Trappe is as close to a hobby as it gets—a place where a few baseball-minded retirees can help Roser run things while schoolkids, American Legion teams—and Harold Baines—can feed tokens into the slot, set their stance, and dream of past and future glory.

It is a big place as indoor batting cages go and that helps, especially in the winter. Outdoor ranges, of course, have the advantage of a real outfield where a batter actually can see how far his best shot goes. Indoors it helps to have high ceilings. To make things more interesting Roser has placed bullseyes at various heights along the back wall. Smack one through this hole and it's a triple; through that one and it's a homer. Through still another and you bat free.

In the winter, and to a baseball freak, it literally is the only game in town.

To anyone who grew up loving the game, an evening of softball at a local field on a summer night—when you are so close to the players that you can hear every exhortation and expletive—is heaven on grass.

This night, in Easton, Md., the Moose Lodge was playing the Bud Lights and before long it was clear the Bud Lights were outclassed.

"C'mon, c'mon, c'mon!" the Bud Light catcher exhorted his players, "Let's pay attention out there."

"That's good concentration," he would say, trying to find something to praise in his teammates. His boosterism was infectious but his team was creamed.

There really wasn't much of a crowd this night but no one seemed to care. The best dressed fans were teenaged girls—friends, one assumes, of the players—gathered to lend support and lead the occasional cheer. The refreshment stand behind home plate in a cramped wooden shack did perfunctory business as spectators chatted and kibitzed and as fireflies flickered in the vanishing light.

There is something about sitting in wooden stands, nursing a beer and eavesdropping on conversations floating on the evening air, that makes watching a smalltown softball game relaxing and satisfying.

So what if the homeplate ump seemed to have an ever-changing strike zone? So what if the Bud Lights couldn't hit out of the infield? It is the slow and regular rhythm of the game that gives baseball—and by extension, softball—its appeal.

You leave humming the tunes.

With their smoky flavor and armor-like exterior, beaten biscuits are an acquired taste. But 89-year-old Ruth Orrell swears she doesn't know why anyone wouldn't love them.

Along with members of her family and a dedicated group of neighbor women, Ruth has been making and selling the hard little doughballs from her home in Wye Mills, Md., since 1935, using virtually the same recipe of flour, lard, water, sugar, salt and baking powder that was used by the colonists. "The harder they are, the better I like 'em," she said as she surveyed the three women and one grandson who this morning were forming the biscuits each in his or her own way and carefully placing them on baking sheets.

Once Ruth literally had to beat the biscuits with a hammer, and later with a hand-cranked machine. She thought she would have to quit in 1960 when her shoulder began to rebel from all the pounding and cranking. But a friend rigged up a mechanical contraption to do the work for her—"the only one like it in the world," she notes proudly. It looks like a cross between a paddlewheel and a paper shredder. Now she can feed a huge mound of dough into the thing and 30 minutes later have the makings for the hardest biscuits you've ever tried to sink your teeth into.

A softspoken man in his 40s, blacksmith Rob Hudson and his wife came to the Eastern Shore, settling in Rock Hall, Md., because land was plentiful and cheap. He not only built his workshop and forge singlehandedly, he also made the nails that hold much of it together.

But simply to call Rob Hudson a blacksmith is to miss the point.

He is more correctly a bladesmith, or Master Smith—in fact, one of only 20 Americans entitled to stamp the letters "M.S." on their work. His forte is knives and at last look his customer waiting list was two and a half years. The patrons who wait this long—and who can pay thousands of dollars for the privilege—often choose Hudson's specialty: a custom designed knife with a Damascus blade.

These remarkable and incredibly sharp blades look as if someone has drawn a delicate and beautiful design along the knifeblade. In fact, the designs are the result of the hundreds of layers of steel Hudson creates in each knife by pounding, then folding over, the molten metal, the better to give the knife flexibility and strength. Immersion in an etching bath reveals the pattern which then becomes a separate work of art. It goes without saying that Hudson carves his own knife handles as well.

The Chincoteague Fire Department has been protecting that island community since the 1930s and today boasts a membership of approximately 100 volunteers, of which 30 are active firefighters.

Police Chief Willis J. Dize, who also served a one-year term as President of the Department, estimated that ambulance and emergency calls outnumber fire calls by about four to one. "There's still more fires than what we'd like," he said, "but I'd say we handle on average about 300-400 ambulance calls a year as opposed to about 50-100 fire calls."

One fire call that hit perilously close to home came a few years ago when the firehouse itself went up. Somehow—the details still are confusing—sewer gas built up under the building and wound up leaking through a sink, where it then ignited. A local photographer caught the action in a series of dramatic color photos showing smoke billowing from the firehouse windows and yellow-jacketed firefighters scurrying to put out the blaze. The photos now adorn the Fire Department's upstairs walls.

For nearly 70 years the Department has supplemented its revenues through the annual Chincoteague Pony Penning and Auction. The summertime event draws thousands to see the famed Chincoteague ponies swim from their habitat on nearby Assateague Island to Chincoteague and trot down the town's main street to the fairgrounds, guided by a phalanx of firemen-turned-cowboys.

There the ponies are auctioned off, with the proceeds going to the Department.

John and Betsy Feiler feel it is a miracle they ended up in Wades Point, Md.—five miles from St. Michaels and so far away from their former life.

Before they opened their bed and breakfast, the Wades Point Inn, their life centered around New York City and John's job as an executive with Revlon, Inc. Then one day the exasperation grew so great for Betsy that she walked to the top of a hill near their suburban home, looked up and said: "Oh God, do whatever you want with me, but get me out of here!"

After briefly considering farming, the Feilers fell in love with the property at Wades Point, owned by the same family since 1819 and operated as an inn since 1890. (The pull of history is strong here. The British attempted a landing near Wades Point during the War of 1812.)

"We both flew through the place," Betsy said, sharing the feeling that they had found the ideal place to settle. "It didn't add up between the ears, but it felt right in the heart."

Once the inn was purchased several years ago, the Feilers began a major renovation and building program. For example, the original house had only three bathrooms for 18 separate bedrooms. In addition, noted John, "the whole place was served by only 100 amps."

Today, renovated and rebuilt, the Inn has become known for two things: its spectacular waterfront view and its restful peace.

And, of course, for the hospitality of a couple of ex-New Yorkers who found their haven on the Eastern Shore and who decided to share it.

"I'm the last of a generation of a hundred years of oystermen," said Richard Waters. In the accent of the region he pronounced it "arstermen."

"I'm the last," he said, then added with a wry grin: "and I'm on my way out too."

Richard and his father, Benjamin Waters, work out of Nanticoke, Md. They rise before dawn with their fellow oystermen to dredge the waters for the delicate sea creature that helps turn the Chesapeake into what Mencken once called "that great protein factory."

But a number of factors including over-harvesting, pollution and zealous conservation rules imposed by the state, have changed things. There simply aren't as many oysters as there were before.

"I don't see in the near future making a decent living off the water," Richard said with resignation. He had returned to the Eastern Shore from Minneapolis, where he had been a social worker, to follow the water. But the water proved a reluctant and difficult partner. For his father, too, life on the Bay has been bittersweet. "I've been on the water, I guess, about 50 years," Ben Waters said. "I wanted to go to college, but I was the first child of eight and I had to help my dad." But, Waters added, "from my experience and everything, I think I've benefited quite a bit from it."

"So I'll be here now until I go for good."

O f the 4,000 hogs on Richard E. Jones' sprawling farm in Pocomoke, Md., a fortunate handful do not have to worry about Monday mornings and the weekly drive to the slaughterhouse. These hefty sows and boars are Jones' breeding stock and their lives amount to a regular regimen of eating, sleeping and making more hogs.

Jones, a strapping man in his 60s, has been raising hogs most of his adult life and he harbors no sentimental feelings about them. They are a source of food, a source of employment, and a source of income.

"The animal righters don't like this," he said, pointing to the tight metal cages that confine nursing sows so that they cannot accidentally crush their young. Jones said he could think of no more practical or humane way to protect the piglets.

In the breeding facility boars and sows are kept in separate pens until the time comes for a team of workers to place a male in among several females, where he will set to work amid much mounting and squealing.

Occasionally, a breeding hog of outgoing nature can make his presence felt even when he's not working. Today, as the operation progressed, this boar—named Flash—raised his 300 pounds upward and snorted greetings to two of Jones' men, Leonard Taylor (l.) and Ron Jarrell. "He's really like a pet," Jarrell said before reaching over to rub Flash on the snout.

Modern taxidermists rarely "stuff" their trophies anymore. Deer, elk, moose and caribou, for example, routinely are mounted on plastic cores over which their skin is fastened by stitch and staple.

These cores are flesh-color and at quick glance they look like hollow-eyed, flayed cadavers. It takes someone with the artistry of Don Travis to bring all the pieces back to life.

Travis, 38, has been mounting animals, birds and fish since he was 20. He occasionally will get a call to preserve a housepet, but his clientele is mostly made up of the hunters and fishermen who live near him in Rock Hall, Md., or who have read about his work in national magazines.

The work is more art than science. Travis' attention to detail—in recreating the musculature on a deer's neck or in capturing the glare of a buck about to charge—is amazing; the result both of study and of observing animals in the wild.

Taxidermy, he explains, means the movement of skin and it is that kind of movement, as he manipulates a mounted hide as a sculptor might mold clay, that turns a dead animal into a work of art.

Though the Eastern Shore is not exactly a melting pot —what with the number of families whose roots go back centuries and who never have left the place—occasionally you get an exuberant new addition like Harry Katsetos of New Church, Va., by way of Greece.

In terms of enthusiasm alone, Harry is a dynamo: a big man with a big heart who thinks nothing of cooking up hundreds of pieces of chicken and donating them to a nearby old people's home. Or who once considered spending Thanksgiving at a local lockup so he could feed chicken to the inmates and visit with them.

Harry's is the classic tale of an immigrant's love for his adopted country: he positively exudes good will as he presides over his Country Kitchen restaurant and pizza parlor at T's Corner near the turnoff to Chincoteague. Harry and his wife Maria came to America and the Eastern Shore several years ago, following Harry's brother George, who had opened his own takeout place several years earlier on Chincoteague.

Sure, it is good p.r. for a restaurant to throw a few free meals around once in a while, but Harry seems to have a hard time turning anybody down. His bulletin board—which he is not bashful about showing off—is cluttered with thank-you notes from schools, churches, organizations and individuals who have been touched by this new American's generosity.

As two visitors wolf down one of Harry's Greek-style pizzas (and try unsuccessfully to turn down some of Maria's baklava), they are shown the only things that can make Harry even prouder than his wall of thank-yous.

They are an armload of his ten-year-old son Peter's gradeschool test papers, nearly every one of which bears a high grade. With typical gusto Harry thrusts the papers at you, his eyes moist. Harry, it seems, can barely read, so he lives his dreams through Peter, and when he impulsively bearhugs his son, you can't help being moved by his joy.

"I had my accident six months before we were married," said Gene Shaffer, "and for the first year I sat around feeling sorry for myself—'Oh I can't go huntin', I can't do this, I can't do that.'"

"Then, finally, Mary came up to me and said, 'Get off your ass; you're gonna hunt.'"

Once a year the Chincoteague Wildlife Refuge stages a controlled hunt to manage and thin out a deer population that flourishes in the sanctuary because of the absence of natural predators. Hunters from all over flock to the refuge, including a sizeable number with disabilities. In fact, the Chincoteague hunt is said to be one of the best and safest venues for hunters in wheelchairs. For the better part of a month in the winter the wildlife refuge is closed to the public during prescribed hours as hunters are permitted to work in designated areas apportioned by a no-nonsense group of U.S. Park Service Rangers headed by Kenny Kessler, a blond-haired Tennesseean who goes over the refuge's strict safety rules during a pre-hunt briefing that all participants must attend.

He notes that the refuge's first commitment is to protect endangered migratory waterfowl, then indigenous wildlife like the plentiful Whitetail deer. Finally, Kessler says, the Park Service permits "recreational activities," including hunting, when there is no threat to the first two. In this case, the non-indigenous and extremely prolific Sika (often called a deer but actually a member of the elk family) must be thinned regularly—even if the idea of a wildlife refuge being turned into a once-a-year killing ground is abhorrent to some.

For those in wheelchairs, the refuge's paved Woodland Trail is perfect. Deep in the sanctuary, the trail provides these hunters with the access they need to hunt successfully. On this day, Gene Shaffer, his wife Mary, and two fellow hunters, George Markland and Tom Reese, bagged their limit during what surely was a perfect day. In fact the only annoyance were two tourists on bicycles who, because of an ambiguous sign at the trail's entrance, pedaled blithely into the hunt area—then hightailed it out when Mary, in flame orange vest and cap, put them right.

Lawson Williams is a farmer who has worked on the Eastern Shore all his life. A large man with a gentle face and a slight stammer, he lives in Marion, Md., with his mother, Miss Emily.

Williams is bothered by arthritis in his knees, aggravated no doubt by his size. Where once he could work in the fields, now he is limited to operating a tractor or some other piece of farm machinery that allows him to sit.

He raises rabbits and when he asks if you would like to see them he springs from his chair with unexpected speed and fetches Sir Walter Raleigh from his metal cage. Sir Walter is a big thing—a stud rabbit—and is as impressive in his way as is his master. But it is the miniature rabbits that create the tenderest, most lasting, image.

Williams holds two in his rotund hands, each meaty palm nearly covering each bunny, and as he talks to you about them he caresses them and smiles. His eyes nearly disappear when he smiles giving Lawson's face the cast of a contented Buddha in baseball cap and coveralls. Still, rabbits are a source of income to Lawson and Miss Emily and he sells them for meat. But when the price of rabbit falls too low, often he simply gives them away.

The slaughter begins in the spotlessly clean kill room 4:30 every Monday morning. Three at a time mature hogs are led into a small holding pen as a man in boots and rubber apron readies a special .22 caliber pistol. So quickly it is hard to see he places the shiny silver gun to a hog's brain. The kill is immediate and the worker quickly puts down the pistol and lunges over the metal fence to slit the throat of the now-convulsing animal. As the two remaining hogs squeal desperately, trying to climb over each other and out of the pen, a river of blood flows onto the angled floor and into the blood drain.

Depending on your point of view, the kill room at Young's Meat Barn in Parksley, Va., is like an efficient auto assembly line or a grisly death chamber. Workers at separate stations do separate jobs as the product—in this case a dead 300-pound hog—moves from one man to the next, hanging by its hind legs from a movable ceiling chain. Within minutes the carcass is scraped smooth, decapitated and sawed down the middle. A state inspector examines every animal before it is allowed to be butchered.

Young's Meat Barn, started 26 years ago by Ralph Young and run now by his son Franklin, is one of the few markets on the Eastern Shore that kills its own meat. That means customers literally can buy sausage and pork chops that 24 hours before was a living animal.

Carlton and Shirley Plummer had their first taste of trailer living shortly after they married in 1947.

"You couldn't get housing then," Shirley said, remembering the time in Wilmington, Del., when her husband was finishing college and when couples starting out in that booming postwar period were willing to try anything. "We bought a little 19-foot trailer—eight feet wide—and lived in it for two years."

"It was like a bunch of gypsies," Carlton said, laughing. "It had no bathroom, you had to go to the showerhouse, but it was exciting. You had ironworkers who were building the Memorial Bridge, TWA pilots..."

"And the jockeys from Delaware Park," Shirley piped in.

The kick of living that way stayed with the Plummers and they spent many summers with like-minded friends camping at various beaches. But when land became available on the Eastern Shore, on Delaware's Broadkill Beach, the Plummers and their friends knew they had found their sandy Xanadu. "We were on the beach and two of our fellas came back and said, 'We found us a place!'" Shirley recalled. "The guy at the store at the time was selling the lots and I think he thought he had a land boom because all ten of us rushed up there and bought ten lots."

Originally, Carlton wanted to put only a trailer shell on their land but Shirley knew it would never be finished. The trailer they finally settled on had wood paneling and was ready to live in. Like many trailer-dwellers on Broadkill Beach, where the now-retired Plummers live fulltime, Carlton and Shirley have added onto theirs with a vengeance. They built a wraparound deck and patio—not to mention the elaborate landscaping with tropical plants and cartoon animal lawn ornaments.

"It's a mobile home," Carlton smiled, "but you only move it once."

Though he certainly looks the part, eighty-seven year old Ed Thornton is not a lifetime Eastern Shoreman. He came east from Indiana in 1928 and wound up in Crisfield, Md., decades ago. He has raised a family and made a living—all his way.

He is alone now, save for a few nearby friends who look out for his needs, and for the people who regularly come to his place looking for bargains, antiques, spare parts and good junk. He passes his days among this stuff, which he has amassed and sorted over decades of serious, some might say compulsive, accumulation.

The rubber hose tree is a case in point. When exactly Ed started saving every auto and garden hose that came his way is unclear, but since virtually all are full of dry rot and since the tree from which they hang is covered with moss, it's a safe bet the collection began a good while back. "I just picked one piece from one place and some from the other," Ed told a visitor matter-of-factly, the implication being that it seemed like a good idea at the time.

His farm—or what once was a farm—is dotted with ancient chestnut trees that regularly drop their gnarly fruit. In an inspiration of necessity mothering invention, Ed places the nuts in the path of his pickup truck whenever he goes on a collecting foray so that whenever he or a friend pulls out, the nuts are cracked open. In addition to providing access for humans, this also creates a wondrous buffet for the squirrels.

A chipper fellow with a smooth face and keen eyes, Ed seems like someone who can get along with anyone. There is someone, though.

"The woman across the road. I shot her dog for killing my chickens and she got on the outs with me."

"Come to think of it, she's still mad at me."

Every year, the Easton, Md., Waterfowl Festival draws thousands of people to this tiny town on the Eastern Shore. In the armory, in school auditoriums, in church basements, people crowd in to see exhibits that celebrate the area and the craftspeople it produces.

Woodcarvers show off their amazingly lifelike birds. Model builders exhibit minutely detailed versions of workboats and other vessels. Bladesmiths offer knives with intricate Damascus blades and handles beautifully inlaid with bone, wood or stone.

In the area of woodcarving especially, the Festival has become far more than a showcase for local talent. In fact, well known carvers from around the country trek to Easton where they know they will find a receptive audience.

Though it is called the waterfowl festival, the main attraction—the ducks and geese the area is known for—are strangely absent.

That's where Paul Garrett comes in.

For years now, Garrett, a gregarious retiree who no longer hunts himself, has used the space next to his daughter's beauty shop to set up a mini-zoo to show folks from away exactly what all the hoopla is about. There behind chicken wire, dozens of ducks and geese quack and honk contentedly while tourists gawk and read Garrett's little signs describing their habits.

"I just thought it was an interesting thing to do," Garrett said, puffing on his pipe and posing on a folding chair with a comical-looking life-size goose pillow that made passersby do a doubletake.

It is dark and chilly, though the weather could be a lot worse, as the hunters gather in the pre-dawn outside Doc's Quick-Shop in Trappe, Md. This morning a large group have paid their money to shoot with Bo Kennedy, one of the best known guides in the region. They are hunting geese and by 6:15 this December morning they are bouncing along in trucks heading for the open cornfields where the fabled honkers are certain to fly.

To the first-timer, the prep work is surprising. First, all hands in this group—three hunters, two guides and one photographer—plant dozens of silhouette birds in the area near the blind, followed by an equal number of stuffed geese, their stiff wired feet attached to weighted platforms. By the time dawn breaks, you'd swear you were standing in the middle of a goose convention. But, of course, that's the idea.

With the prep work done and the sun peering through, guides Tim Lyons and Tony Adams set to work attracting the geese. Both men work their goose calls (each has a favorite one; each has a slightly different sound.) Tim acts as the main observer while the hunters stay huddled out of sight in the grass-covered blind. When a group of birds approaches Tim spots them first.

"Coming from the left, over the trees," he might say, as Tony, on his knees just outside the blind, waves a black flag back and forth. The sound approximates that of wings and the back and forth motion is supposed to attract the hungry birds.

If all succeeds—if the multiple subterfuges of the blind, the camouflage-covered hunters, the goose calls, the decoys and the waving flag work—one or more geese will suddenly "lock up" their wings and glide silently down to join the other "geese" on the ground.

It is then that Tim yells "Take them!" and three hunters jump up and empty their guns into the sky.

In the gentle windowlight, Helen Gaskins wields her needle with quiet ease. The quilts that bear her name easily can fetch more than a thousand dollars apiece.

She was a fixture among—in fact, had been the president of—the loose confederation of Chincoteague, Va., women who met weekly behind the Union Baptist Church for their regular quilting bee. A first time visitor could be forgiven for assuming that Helen has been quilting all her life.

In fact, she has been doing it only a couple of years, her natural talent as a needlewoman emerging only after she tried a tentative hand at piecing multiple squares and triangles of fabric into her first quilt.

"If you can piece like that, you can also quilt," a friend said, and shortly thereafter Helen became the quilt lady of Chincoteague.

"We do take in a couple or three thousand dollars a year," she said. "We gave, I think it was, over twelve hundred dollars last year to the church's mission."

Quilts by Helen and her fellow quilters are offered for sale at bazaars, fairs and other social events on Chincoteague. A sure fundraiser is a raffle of one of Helen's quilts, especially one with a seasonal or holiday motif.

"We don't keep any of the money for ourselves," Helen declared. "But we do take a trip to Ocean City once a year."

Crisfield, Md., once referred to as Dodge City by the Sea, was—and in some ways remains—a rough place with hard edges, as hard as the millions of oyster shells on which several city blocks of Crisfield stand.

Until 1873, the city had no jailhouse. According to local historian Col. Woodrow T. Wilson, a temporary lockup was a railroad boxcar until the town finally built a proper jailhouse. Today locals will tell you that things have improved, but they are quick to note that, given the city's past, there was plenty of room for improvement.

One such improvement may be Clarence Bell, the first black ever to be named Chief of Police. The mere fact that an African-American could hold such a position speaks volumes about social change in an area that had resisted such change for decades. Bell's elevation came after his predecessor was forced out of office amidst allegations of criminal conduct. Bell seems anxious not only to solidify his support among Crisfield's sizeable black population but to make inroads into its white population as well. Hence an almost endless round of rubber chicken dinners and civic appearances: the brick and mortar of what he hopes will be acceptance.

Up Creek Alley on Little Creek in Chester, Md., sits David Wehr's seafood factory. From the outside it is a large, clean modern place where trucks arrive dockside every day to load up on crabs, pollock, shrimp and other seafood that is then trucked to area restaurants and stores. Inside, too, the bustle of a thriving business is evident in the huge pressure cookers that steam thousands of crabs at a time, producing the spicy delicacy for which so much of Maryland is known. One story up, in woodpaneled offices, buyers negotiate price over the phone with local watermen.

But wander further inside the factory and the businesslike bustle competes with culture shock: for the large room devoted solely to crab-picking might easily be, not in Chester, Maryland, but in Phnom Penh, Cambodia.

The workers who so diligently pluck the Maryland blue crab are almost all Cambodian. They are young, old, male and female. They are bused in every day from their homes in Silver Spring, Md., and provide Wehr's and other seafood plants with a steady and reliable workforce. It is not difficult to imagine the odyssey that brought them here: leaving a war-torn country for the comparative security of Silver Spring's growing and close-knit Cambodian and Vietnamese community.

Paid by the pound they work with speed and determination, though chatter and laughter occasionally puncture the atmosphere. At break time there is no klatch by the water cooler. Instead, one sees men and women seated on their haunches brewing tea over a sterno stove.

In a region where painstakingly carved handcrafted ducks can command hundreds of dollars apiece, this man is making 48 duck heads at a time. He is operating the custom-made multiple lathe at Stoney Point Decoy Factory, said to be the largest such facility in the world, on Route 13 in Oak Hall, Va. (In point of fact, the man is working with only 24 pieces of wood as he guides a stylus over a metal template—separate drill bits do the actual carving. But each of the 24 wood pieces makes two duck heads, one upside down, one right side up, beaks touching.)

It began as a garage business nearly 20 years ago and has grown steadily since, though few hunters today use wooden decoys. "Nowadays, most of them use decoys made of cork, or inflatable ones—all of them cheap," noted Monty Lightfoot, Stoney Point's sales manager. Occasionally, Lightfoot adds, "some of the more affluent hunters" will order wooden decoys, but the bulk of Stoney Point's production of ducks, geese and swans is decorative.

In the cavernous factory a fine mist of sawdust is barely discernible at first, but quickly becomes obvious as it covers everything and everyone. The fine particles come from the band sanders where workers, mostly women, put the finishing touches on the wooden birds before they are painted. At quitting time, men and women give themselves a long onceover with a high pressure air hose before punching out and heading home.

Lightfoot, a genial, eager-to-please fellow, was asked what he would say to someone who looked down his nose at Stoney Point's mass produced birds in favor of a master carver's one-of-a-kind variety.

"I would say: 'he carves ducks; we carve decoys.'"

For some, living on the Eastern Shore means living apart from the faster, more hectic, pace west of the Bay Bridge. For artist Regina Hall it also has meant growing in touch with a world of color she never had known before.

It is a regular part of their day for Regina and her husband, publisher Jonathan Hall, to wander the wooded paths of the Chincoteague wildlife refuge and the Assateague national seashore, and breathe in the clean air and enjoy the tranquil world of these carefully tended havens. The couple had come to the Eastern Shore from Washington, DC, in 1987 to open the Main Street Gallery on Chincoteague and for Jonathan to begin publishing newsletters for the water industry. Before coming to the Shore (they had lived for a while in Baltimore and New York as well), Regina's work "tended to be dark and abstract. But within a short time after we moved here, suddenly color entered my work."

The change, she believes, was triggered by those walks in the woods: seeing how the forest was really made up of hundreds of shades of green, how the trees themselves were composed of, not one or two, but dozens of colors.

Finally, she recalled, one night while staring at a blank wall, she envisioned an abstract, ladderlike form made from the pieces of vine and branches that she and Jonathan collected during their walks—but all painted bright colors.

"The next day I made my first ladder," followed shortly thereafter by the cruciform shown here, awash in turquoise and green and cradled by Assateague vines painted in complementary tranquil shades.

"That piece has to do with the spiritual kind of feeling I get about Assateague," Regina said. "I couldn't have done it anywhere but here."

Christine and Dale Johnson, shown here with their daughter Kelsey and 27,000 chickens, did not start out to be farmers—much less the largest organic farmers on the Eastern Shore.

"It was totally unplanned," Christine said in the tenacious accent of her native New York City. "Originally, we were academics—we both taught college. But we always enjoyed growing things. Even in New York, whenever I could get my hands in the dirt, I did."

Christine and Dale began to farm in 1985, but tentatively. Having bought a ten-acre spread in Marion, Md., Dale continued to commute to Rutgers, where he taught sociology, while Christine took on the farming chores fulltime.

"But when Kelsey came along we realized there wasn't much security in vegetables—it's a very high risk business—so we invested in another chicken house." That investment more than doubled their capacity and allowed the Johnsons to raise 50,000 chickens at a time for—whom else?—Frank Perdue.

Perdue's folksy ads notwithstanding, chicken farming is a tough, unromantic business. Ironically, given its nature, it also is as bloodless as any big business can be. Dale notes that Perdue allows for a 3% mortality rate among the 50,000 chicks it delivers every 6-8 weeks for the Johnsons to grow. The slightest rise in that rate—say up to 4% owing to an outbreak of disease—and Perdue's people grow unhappy to the point, Dale says, of threatening to withdraw their business.

It makes for a testy and tentative relationship with a major employer on the Eastern Shore, one whose shadow looms large not only over chicken growers, but also over the men and women who produce the corn and soybeans that help make up Perdue's "secret" blend of poultry feed.

Hunter Peacock ran his hands over the old chair, pulling apart an already tattered seam, and looked inside. He liked what he saw.

"They don't build 'em like this anymore," he said, echoing thousands of car, camera, train and who knows how many other kinds of buffs who have sadly watched the workmanship that goes into making their favorite things deteriorate over time.

Gingerly, but with more confidence, Peacock pulled open the back of the chair—one of a pair of art deco loungers that seemed to have been born to grace a movie palace. "See what I mean?" he exulted as he pointed out the sturdy wood frame that seemed to underpin every part of the forlorn yet still impressive looking chair.

Yes, it was agreed that the two chairs would be remade. After all, they had been bought for a song in Pocomoke City, Md., and to have them reborn at Eastern Shore Upholstery just a few miles away in New Church, Va., seemed reasonable, if not wonderfully appropriate. The search for fabric was difficult since it was impossible to duplicate the original plush, but a suitable velvet was substituted.

The chairs turned out beautifully.

Some months later a friend who had grown up in Washington, DC, saw the reborn chairs and completed the circle. She said she was sure these were the same chairs she remembered as a child sitting in the lobby of one of Washington's famed—and now long-gone—movie palaces. It felt good to bring them back home again.

Though only a comparatively short way from Cambridge, Md., and accessible by car via bridges and causeways, Hooper's Island, Md., gives the feeling of being a remote place. Flat, as is so much of the Eastern Shore, Hooper's impresses with its vistas and its beautiful sunsets. It's hard to get lost since there is only one main road. Modest clapboard homes dot the island and the docks are filled not with yachts but with workboats.

In the midst of this—or more precisely, at the end of this and fronting on the Chesapeake—is the Hooper's Island Gun Club, the euphemism for the island getaway of Bill and Agnes Doeller of Warrenton, Va. Acres of unspoiled marshland at the end of the island create the perfect place to hunt duck. Strategically placed blinds dot the acreage and those fortunate enough to be invited for a several-day stay never forget either the hunting or the hospitality.

The base of operations is the Doeller's spacious home, and at its core the warm, woodpaneled living room and huge fireplace. The daily regimen is not hard to take: Up at dawn for the morning hunt, then back at midday for a gourmet lunch. Then a nap in your room, followed by the afternoon hunt that continues till sundown. Dinner, not surprisingly, often is duck.

In the old days, the tradition was that the final dinner was black tie. But that has given way to less formal times, and business dress now replaces the afternoon's rubber boots and camouflage suits.

Paul Long is a backyard mechanic near Marion, Md., with so florid a face that it prompts the nickname "Beet."

His backyard is a collection of derelict cars and trucks that he cannibalizes for parts as he works with his son Mike. Together they help local farmers and others stretch, retool, and jury-rig their machinery, cars and appliances to keep them going one more season.

It is not at all unusual for someone's terminal car engine to wind up partially reincarnated as, say, a winch or a pump. Or for someone with a broken machine to find just the part he needs amidst Paul and Mike's collection of good mechanical junk.

Long is one of those people who greets strangers with a bemused smile rather than suspicion. He enjoys pulling your leg, too, and the sound of laughter is never far away. Back in his field, behind the two open-sided barns that serve as Long's shop, is an old green schoolbus that honks. It honks because Paul has removed the seats and turned the bus into a coop for his chickens and one imperious goose.

In a small community the business of running the school system often covers things much more mundane—and sometimes much more important—than introducing reluctant pupils to learning.

This unseasonably warm Spring morning in Princess Anne, Md., H. DeWayne Whittington, school board superintendent of Somerset County, had just come to work and was dealing with two prickly issues: a teacher whose contract was not being renewed and a school bus that had just broken down.

The former was, in some ways, the easier to confront. Whittington, who grew up on the Eastern Shore and whose reputation as an educator extends far beyond the region, clearly felt he could not retain someone whose performance was below par. The bus was another matter. As a staff member relayed the bad news, Whittington tried to think of ways to get another bus in his meager fleet to do the work of two. Any alternative meant one group of students had to do without: a field trip missed; a ride home delayed.

For the remainder of the time that Whittington was being photographed he pored over papers or spoke on the phone, lost in the often-maddening minutiae of his job. The only time he looked up was when he was asked to face the camera. When he did he wasn't smiling.

"Miz Annie" Parks, 91, a rugged survivor with an enchanting smile, is the matriarch of Tangier Island, Va.

Known to everyone on the tiny island, she is a living keeper of the history of this remarkable place and delights in welcoming visitors, even strangers, into her home. Her living room, warmed by a propane stove and guarded by an old sleepy lab, is crammed with pictures of her two children, nine grandchildren, 16 great grandchildren—and seven great great grandchildren.

"We all know each other," Miz Annie said of her friends and neighbors. "When one gets in trouble the whole island is in trouble."

She was married in 1920 and, of course, her husband was also from the island and, of course, he was a waterman. "He'll be gone 29 years," Miz Annie said matter-of-factly, since she is not one to dwell on the past. Her memory goes back to the time when the population was not as concentrated as it now must be. The once-scattered "Tangierines" now live on one of three "ridges" connected by a series of foot bridges and paved roads too small for automobiles. Erosion and the ravages of foul weather have made areas like the far south end of Tangier, beyond the ruggedly beautiful Cod Harbor, uninhabitable.

Change and "progress" have exacted other tolls. Author Tom Horton wrote that "the white picket fences I recalled (have) been supplanted by chain link, giving the island's one narrow main street the look of a dog kennel run."

But that can't alter the pull Tangier has on its people. What makes the island so special? Miz Annie is asked.

"I guess 'cause it's home," she replied smiling.

Academics often are pegged as people with arcane or specialized knowledge of their fields. They have nothing on antique dealers. It can be a nomadic existence, riding from one antique show to the next: to buy, to sell, to size up the market for a particular piece. But to those it suits, there can be no other life.

Mole and Kay Early's cavernous antique shop sits among an assortment of businesses along route 13 near the turnoff to Chincoteague, and epitomizes the notion that today's castoffs are tomorrow's treasures. Though located on the Eastern Shore, Early's Antiques features little that is exclusively Shore-related—save for an impressive array of beautifully decorated oyster cans that command big bucks from collectors. Their speciality is early American: from pie safes to hook rugs to rough-hewn furniture to hand-wrought tools that show the warmth and wear of decades of use.

Some time ago a woman brought in an old curved horn and asked Mole if he knew what it might have been used for. "It might have been a powder horn," he conjectured. But since a good antiques dealer must be a combination archeologist, history buff and raconteur he could not rule out a friend's suggestion that it might also have been a shofar, the ceremonial instrument made from a ram's horn and used by Jews to mark the beginning of the high holy days.

On Main Street in Chincoteague, Va., folks who need artificial flowers or Christmas ornaments, or who want to learn how to make them, have the Painted Pony Craft Shop. There amid hot glue, paint, pipe cleaners and styrofoam is Connie Connor to set them right about their decoupage and decorated eggs.

Connie, a New Jersey native—as are many who gravitate to the Eastern Shore—runs the Painted Pony with a breezy, informal manner that makes friends easily. She jokes about the demands each holiday places upon her. Like clothing stores selling the fall line as temperatures soar, Connie prepares painted Santas and Christmas wreaths as tourists traipse through town in Bermuda shorts.

To meet Connie and her husband Chuck is also to meet their dog Puggy. He is, of course, a Pug—a short thing with a pushed-in face and consequent snorfling and wheezing. As dogs go, Puggy is no beauty, but he makes up for it with personality.

"He'll smile for the picture, really," Connie said as she and Chuck posed in matching recliners in their living room above the store. On command, Puggy hopped onto the arm of Connie's chair and flashed what for him was a 100-watter. When Connie and Chuck's two cats had the temerity to wander into the room during the photo session, Puggy hopped down onto the floor, scared the hell out of them, then hopped back onto the arm of Connie's recliner—and smiled.

You could almost hear him say, "Take Two."

The Garden and the Sea Inn, perhaps the most elegant restaurant and inn on the Eastern Shore, found its inspiration in the south of France when Victoria Olian and her husband Jack Betz, harried after 20 years of "high-stress city-type jobs," fell in love with Provence and decided to change their lives.

"We love to travel in France and we spent a summer there in '86, in the south of France, in a very tiny town near Aix-en-Provence," Vicky recalled. The summer provided the two with their first extended vacation in years—Jack was at the time a real estate attorney in Washington; she had an interior design business—and both were fascinated by the simple yet elegant mom and pop inns they frequented.

"The French are probably the princes of hospitality in the world in terms of their establishments: food and drink and all that kind of thing, and we thought that having a place of some graciousness, to provide lodging and good food and a pleasant environment—a welcome respite—was something that appealed to us."

Vicky is the chef de cuisine, working with only a handful of helpers in a cramped kitchen, to turn locally grown produce and meats into glorious meals. Jack acts as host and innkeeper. It can be grueling, and a far cry from the bucolic vacation existence they knew in France. But it suits them.

The couple had hoped to open Garden and the Sea on Chincoteague, where they had vacationed for 14 years, but couldn't find the right site. Finally, when a somewhat dilapidated but still beautiful Victorian became available near New Church, Va., they set to work renovating and rebuilding. They opened for business April 1, 1989 and, though exhausted by the end of each season, they have never looked back.

She was planning to go to law school—had apprenticed with a lawyer in Salisbury—but Charlene Upham of Mardela, Md., had antiques in her blood.

"I was going to go to law school in Tulsa," she said, "but I took a summer off and went into the flea market business instead. Sold real low-end things like Depression glass and oak furniture—anything I could get my hands on.

"That was back in the late 70s, when things were really booming, and I just loved it and never went to law school. I did shows for about five years. By that time, you had such a huge investment in time and money and, of course, inventory."

As she spoke, Charlene posed among some of her prized antique dolls, her own flowing curls mimicking those on some of her "inventory." Her parents, she noted, have an antique shop just down the road, "so I'm a second generation antiques dealer."

Her claim to the Eastern shore is much stronger. "My mother's people have been on the Eastern Shore since the late 17th century. The Wheatleys and the Brinsfields—old Dorchester county names."

In Pocomoke City, Md., which bills itself as the friendliest town on the Eastern Shore, farmer Keith Chesser had his store—and his deer. The deer was shot by Chesser's son Donnie. Clearly, the taxidermy job was less than the best.

Before illness forced him to close down, Chesser catered to a largely poor and black clientele. He sold fish and what small game local hunters brought in. Fortified wine and beer rounded out his modest inventory.

Pocomoke City wasn't always so friendly. In the 60s, and even not too many years ago, Chesser recalled that blacks were routinely hassled by the police on the streets outside the store. If his customer bought a beer in a paper bag and tried to drink it there was usually hell to pay if a white cop saw him. It never happened to whites, Chesser said.

Finally, he said, he complained to the state and pressure was put on the police to stop. You might not expect an older white man from Pocomoke City to get involved in something like this. But it didn't matter to Chesser.

"It just wasn't right," he said.

"The young ones are the toughest," noted Connie Conder who, with her mother Leone Salyer, runs Chincoteague's oldest and largest funeral home.

"We buried a 17-year-old that died of cancer. There was a 21-year-old who died in a motorcycle accident and someone who would have been 30 fell off his boat this year."

"And there was the 16-, no, 15-year-old that was killed on a skateboard," Leone added.

"Grabbed hold of the side of a pickup truck and went underneath it and the wheels caught him," Connie said.

The main viewing room of Salyer's Funeral Home has the feeling of someone's living room, save for a large oil painting of a praying Jesus that dominates one wall and two great white pillars standing in one corner. The pillars were found by Leone's late husband, who opened the funeral home in the 1950s. He thought the pillars would be perfect for the viewing room and his widow and daughter speak fondly of the day they were installed. The room's other decor is properly somber: dark paneling, overstuffed chairs and deep red carpeting.

In a small place like Chincoteague, a funeral home is more than a business; it is an integral part of the community. With no daily local paper, Salyer's is one of the town's few sources of public death notification. So, in a tradition all but forgotten elsewhere, the funeral home posts the names of the newly dead on a bulletin board on its front door, where passersby walking or riding along Church Street can check the roll.

"We do have the radio now," Connie said. But she noted that the local station charges to have death notices broadcast.

"In the beginning, starting out, it was free, but now they charge."

If the Eastern Shore is a special place, set apart from the "mainland" by a great bridge, how separate must be Tangier Island, Va., itself so isolated from the Eastern Shore.

Accessible only by boat, Tangier is the final tiny island in the middle of the Lower Chesapeake. It is so remote that many on the Eastern Shore never have gone there themselves, yet no part of the Shore may be more demanding of a visit. The first English settlement there was in the late 1600s and today's inhabitants still speak in the up and down cadences of Devon and Cornwall. It is a flat, marshy place, with narrow roads too small for automobiles so locals get about on bikes or in golf carts featuring homemade cabs made of particle board and plywood. Family plots dot Tangier Island, virtually all of them above ground because of the high water table. It is common on the island—sitting in the Bay almost equidistant from the Eastern and Western shores, barely seven feet above sea level—to find gravesites squeezed into front and back yards, surrounded by chain link fence and crowded among swing sets and basketball hoops. With barely two and a half square miles of land, buffeted by the sea and losing a battle with erosion, Tangier is an island where space is a luxury and where the dead are buried wherever they can be.

Today a man in a Washington Redskins hat and sweatshirt brushed white paint over one grave cover. "It's my brother," the man said as he brushed.

"He drownded."

The fact of sudden death is accepted here, where men work the water no matter the weather. The man with the paintbrush—he said his name was John—finally volunteered that he never actually met his brother; he had died that long ago.

"All I know is he's my brother," John said, dipping his brush into the can once more.

THE PHOTOGRAPHER AND THE PHOTOGRAPHS

Frank Van Riper is a commercial and fine art photographer, author, and former newspaper reporter. He had been White House correspondent and national political correspondent of the New York Daily News before leaving journalism for photography in 1987. A former Nieman Fellow at Harvard, he is author of the nationally acclaimed biography, *Glenn: The Astronaut Who Would Be President* (Harper & Row), and holds the 1980 Merriman Smith Award for his presidential news coverage. He is represented in Washington by Touchstone Gallery and is a member of the board of the mid-Atlantic chapter of the American Society of Magazine Photographers. He lives in Washington, DC, with his wife and partner, photographer Judith Goodman.

All portraits in this project were made with Hasselblad cameras and lenses: the 500 C/M using 50mm, 80mm and 150mm lenses, as well as the Superwide C/M.

Lighting depended on the circumstances: from available window light (Keith Chesser and his deer; quilter Helen Gaskins), to ambient light augmented by handheld flash (Ed Thornton; Richard and Benjamin Waters), to more elaborate setups with studio strobe units and reflectors (bladesmith Rob Hudson; Rev. Hattie Ewell).

By project's end virtually all photographs were made on Ilford XP-2 film, for its tight grain and remarkable exposure latitude. Earlier images had been made on Kodak T-Max 100, Kodak Professional Tri-X and on Ilford XP-1. All negatives were processed by StarLab Photographic Services of Bethesda, Maryland.

The photographs were printed by the photographer on Portriga Rapid Glossy, grades 2 or 3, using a Beseler 4x5 enlarger with a Zone VI cold light head.

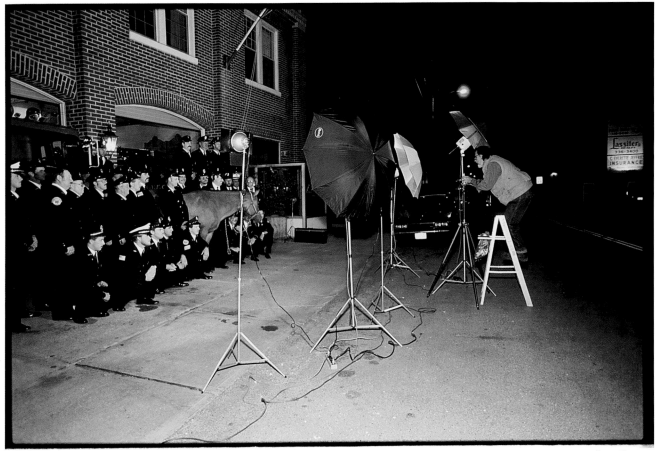

JUDITH GOODMAN

INDEX TO PHOTOGRAPHS

Cover: Keith B. Chesser/Pocomoke, Md.

9. Oyster Shucking/Crisfield, Md.

11. Ira Hudson and Sambo/ Chincoteague, Va.

12. Randy Hudson / Chincoteague, Va.

13. Ira and Frances Hudson/ Chincoteague, Va.

15. Lloyd L. Simpkins / Princess Anne, Md.

17. John Austin Ellsworth / Lewes, Del.

19. Rev. Hattie M. Ewell / Pocomoke City, Md.

21. Passion Play rehearsal, Salisbury Baptist Temple / Salisbury, Md.

22. Last Supper - Passion Play / Salisbury, Md.

23. Crucifixion - Passion Play / Salisbury, Md.

24. William (Corky) Corkell / Felton, Del.

25. William Paskey / Felton, Del.

27. Trish Evans / Pocomoke City, Md.

29. Scorchy Tawes / Salisbury, Md.

31. "Sports Trappe" Batting Cage / Trappe, Md.

33. Evening Softball Game / Easton, Md.

34. Biscuit Making / Wye Mills, Md.

35. Ruth Orrell / Wye Mills, Md.

37. Rob Hudson / Rock Hall, Md.

39. Volunteer Fire Deptartment / Chincoteague, Va.

41. John & Betsy Feiler, Wades Point Inn, Wades Point, Md.

42. Richard & Benjamin Waters / Nanticoke, Md.

43. Richard & Benjamin Waters / Nanticoke, Md.

45. Leonard Taylor, Ron Jarrell and Flash / Pocomoke, Md.

47. Don Travis / Chestertown, Md.

49. Harry Katsetos / New Church, Va.

51. Wheelchair Hunters / Chincoteague, Va.

53. Lawson Williams / Marion, Md.

55. Denuding freshly slaughtered hog, Young's Meat Barn / Parksley, Va.

56. Sawing carcass before butchering, Young's Meat Barn / Parksley, Va.

57. Removing hog jowels, Young's Meat Barn / Parksley, Va.

59. Carlton and Shirley Plummer / Broadkill Beach, Del.

61. Ed Thornton / Crisfield, Md.

63. Paul Garrett / Easton, Md.

64. Waterfowl Exhibit / Easton, Md.

65. Tony Adams, Hunting Guide / Trappe, Md.

67. Goose Hunters at Dawn / Trappe, Md.

69. Helen Gaskins / Chincoteague, Va.

71. Chief C. Edward Bell / Crisfield, Md.

73. Cambodian Crab Pickers, Wehr's Seafood / Chester, Md.

75. Decoy Maker/ Stoney Point Decoy Factory / Oak Hall, Va.

77. Regina Hall / Chincoteague, Va.

79. Christine, Dale and Kelsey Johnson / Marion, Md.

81. Hunter Peacock / New Church, Va.

82. En Route to Duck Blind / Hooper's Island, Md.

83. Hooper's Island Gun Club / Hooper's Island, Md.

85. Paul Long / Marion, Md.

86. H. DeWayne Whittington / Princess Anne, Md.

87. H. DeWayne Whittington / Princess Anne, Md.

89. Annie K. (Miz Annie) Parks / Tangier Island, Va.

91. Mole & Kay Early / New Church, Va.

93. Chuck and Connie Connor with Puggy / Chincoteague, Va.

95. Victoria Olian and Jack Betz, Garden and the Sea Inn / New Church, Va.

97. Charlene Upham / Mardela, Md.

99. Keith B. Chesser / Pocomoke City, Md.

101. Leone Salyer, Connie Conder / Chincoteague, Va.

103. Grave Tending / Tangier Island, Va.

105. Author photographing Chincoteague Fire Department

108. Author / Tangier Island

Back Cover: Leonard Taylor, Ron Jarrell and Flash / Pocomoke, Md.

JUDITH GOODMAN